Choosing Joy for Lent

Marilyn Norquist Gustin

LIGUORI
PUBLICATIONS

One Liguori Drive
Liguori, Missouri 63057-9999
(314) 464-2500

Imprimi Potest:
James Shea, C.SS.R.
Provincial, St. Louis Province
The Redemptorists

Imprimatur:
Monsignor Maurice F. Byrne
Vice Chancellor, Archdiocese of St. Louis

ISBN 0-89243-331-0
Library of Congress Catalog Card Number: 90-70803

Copyright © 1990, Marilyn J. Gustin
Printed in U.S.A.

Cover and Interior Design: Pam Hummelsheim
Cover Photo: Comstock

Contents

Introduction

"I have told you this so that my joy might be in you and your joy might be complete" (John 15:11).

Jesus spoke these words to his disciples on the last evening he spent with them before the crucifixion. Jesus already knew he was going to die (John 13:1). What kind of joy could he have meant? What joy could Jesus have experienced and given fully to his followers while facing his death? Let us not be too quick to say, "Well, he knew about the Resurrection." The answer is more profound and more stimulating.

There is a joy present whose source is far deeper than any circumstances. Jesus knew that joy. A well-known writer has said, "Christ, ...when beaten and when hanging on the cross, experienced all this in his outer man, while the inner man, the soul...rested in the same bliss and joy as it did after the Ascension or as it does at this very moment."[1]

Jesus lived constantly in this joy of union with God. His own abiding, living joy he wished for all his followers. He taught throughout his public life to enable others to experience that very joy.

This deeper joy touches many people unexpectedly. Consider these illustrations. A woman attends a concert when she would rather be resting. She is exhausted, and this particular evening the songs make her sad. She tries to distance herself from her tiredness by trying to experience the music's effect within herself. Suddenly, as if a firecracker bursts in her chest, she is filled with joy, a stabbing, totally unexpected joy that races through her whole being. It is not connected to anything, least of all her restless body or the sad music. Joy simply streams through her heart.

A man walks at night, bent over with sorrow. He wonders despairingly what he is doing here, why his life is such a mess, whether he can ever get out of his present situation. Without warning, joy blazes up in his heart like a fire in full flame. Unreasonably, he is totally alive with dynamic joy. It continues for hours. His troubles are not changed — but he is.

A woman awakens reluctantly, as usual, stumbling at first with the difficulty of navigating in the dark. Somewhere between the bed and the shower she feels a flowing rush of delight and enjoyment flooding her body, so strong that she almost dances with it. It does not go away, and for three days she lives in unbroken joy.

Each of these stories is true. Are experiences like these common? I am sure they are much more common than we usually think because, as a friend said to me, "Joy is socially unacceptable." For some reason people do not talk easily about such experiences. It is so strange that people speak of sorrow but seldom about joy.

But wouldn't you like to have them happen to you? Perhaps such experiences have already occurred in your life. If so, you may wonder how to get them back. If joy has not happened, you may wish you knew how to help such experiences be part of life. Better yet, what if we could live in a constant current of such joy, as Jesus did?

That is what this book is about: preparing ourselves to experience joy, joy so deep and free that it is almost beyond the grasp of all unpleasant circumstances.

We cannot create this joy possessively. In reality, this quality called joy belongs to God and remains his gift. We never control it, yet we can influence our own readiness for it. There is much that we can do, probably even must do, to open ourselves, to prepare ourselves, to receive God's joy within.

Why should the choosing of joy be a good topic for Lent? The answer is simple: because the efforts the Church asks us to make during Lent can be practices that prepare us to become utterly joyful people.

The Purpose of Lent

What attitudes do we already have about Lent and its purposes?

One recent Lenten Sunday my husband and I met a friend we had not seen for a couple of years. After a happy exchange of updating, he said smilingly, "Well, have a miserable Lent!"

Some years ago I worked at a retreat center. Betty, a frequent and enjoyable visitor, came especially often during one Lent. We all knew she had undertaken a challenging discipline: she had given up coffee for Lent — and coffee was her "get-me-through-the-day" habit. The Easter Vigil ended about one o'clock on Easter morning and we all went to the dining room for breakfast. Betty headed straight for the coffee table, took a whole pot, and sat down literally hugging it until dawn. She laughed at herself but loved her coffee.

We so easily fall into the notion that Lent is some teeth-gritting, miserable discipline to be endured for the days of Lent and then abandoned immediately on Easter morning. With such an attitude, effort easily becomes superficial, unconvincing, and boring. The genuine power of Lent is lost to us.

Lent is, rather, for particular attention to an aspect of ourselves that we would like to see changed — preferably a change that would endure. To that end, our efforts and the grace of the Holy Spirit combine in a definite transformation. Our Lenten transformation then becomes one step in a long series of changes that finally creates us completely new. And, as Saint Paul said, all that matters is that one is created anew. (See Galatians 6:15.)

The Church offers us a special season to reflect lovingly on the trials of Jesus' life so that we will feel his companionship in our efforts to become more like him. Intensity is hard to maintain. Forty days is about enough for one time. Yet whatever we practice during Lent is to be aimed at a permanent change.

We are guided quite clearly by the liturgy of Ash Wednesday. At the preface of the Mass, we pray, "Each year you give us this joyful season when we prepare to celebrate the paschal mystery with mind and heart renewed....As we recall the great events that gave us new life in Christ, you bring the image of your Son to perfection in us."

This may be a totally new idea, but Lent is a joyful season. Its purpose is not mere "sticking it out" but a fuller likeness to Christ.

The Christian looks forward to Easter. Easter is not just a memory of a past event. By Jesus' Resurrection the present experience of continuing resurrection after each little death is opened to us. Easter empowers the new creation in us. This is the transformation of our lives, our very ways of being. It is the work of the Holy Spirit.

At the Last Supper, Jesus had said, "But I tell you the truth, it is better for you that I go. For if I do not go, the Advocate will not come to you. But if I go, I will send him to you" (John 16:7). So Jesus, by dying and revealing the Resurrection, is completely united again with the Father and sends the Holy Spirit to us. The Spirit comes for many wonderful purposes, but the goal of them all is to make us like Christ so that we can be joyfully one with him.

If we do not wish to cooperate with this transformational process, to give both our cheerful assent and our strong efforts to the Spirit's work, no one will ever force us to it. God in Christ invites — sometimes urgently and always persistently — but he never forces. Full participation in Lent is a magnificent method of cooperating if we wish.

It is my hope that each reader will find in these pages motivation for such cooperation. The wonderful teaching and help I have received and the discoveries I've been given demand to be shared. One thing I say for certain: no more joyful adventure exists on this earth than cooperation with the transforming work of the Holy Spirit within ourselves. Every Lent is the perfect time to set out afresh.

It is suggested that you read through this whole book once before the beginning of Lent. By doing this you will gain an overall perspective on fresh possibilities for the living of your own Lent. You will be able to choose your own particular practices for this blessed season by using the detailed guidance offered here.

When Easter comes at the end of Lent, we will rejoice with Saint Symeon, who in the tenth century wrote:

Easter, that joyful day...happens daily and eternally in those who know its mystery, and so has filled our hearts with unspeakable joy and gladness....It has perfected our souls and encouraged them as well....Let us therefore give thanks to the Lord, who has brought us over the sea of Lent and led us with joy into the harbor of his Resurrection.[2]

CHAPTER 1

Joy Is Possible

Joy brings a bright glow to our inner being and makes everything seem wonderful. It makes dark days bright; it turns long nights into short ones. Joy may be deep, quiet, solid. It may rush and flow dynamically. Joy is always a splendid experience.

What makes people joyful? We find ordinary joys in several circumstances. Joy comes from getting and having. New things, good relationships, fine work, all stimulate happy feelings. Joy can come from anticipation. There is great pleasure in having "something to look forward to." Joy can come from accomplishment, from achieving a desired goal. That satisfaction affirms the goodness of our efforts. Joy may come from the sudden release of tension, as might happen when a burden is suddenly lifted. We find joy in giving; everyone knows the happiness of offering a kindness to another. Joy comes to the lives of individuals in hundreds of different shapes, sizes, and experiences.

Over time, however, if we observe our lives, we notice that joys, like the examples mentioned above, do not last. They come, perhaps intensely, and then they fade into nothingness. Moreover, they are tied to the pleasures experienced or felt in particular circumstances. If the circumstances change, the pleasurable feeling we have is more than likely to change with them. Because of that we may become glued to the situation that first brought a certain joy. We try to create that event again. Yet what gave us joy then may not do so now. Joys that depend on circumstances come and pass away.

If we watch ourselves, we also find that these joys may become twisted into self-centeredness and pride. Too easily people may take credit for the pleasure or the virtue of the experience. We sometimes think that we are the creator of these joys. We begin to imagine that we can control our lives so as to control our happiness. We may take a joy so for granted that we do not feel any gratitude.

From the viewpoint of spiritual growth, pleasurable experiences run the risk of bringing more self-centeredness to the person and less attention to God. Of course, this need not happen. Pleasures are God's gifts, and many are related to particular situations. When we accept these with happy gratitude, they connect us more to God. We choose the attitude we will take.

Divine Joy

Yet we want to remember that there is a more wonderful intensity of joy, a joy that is stronger. It does not depend on any particular circumstance but comes of itself. It can last, and no situation whatever can block it. Only we ourselves can do that by closing our hearts.

This joy is deeper than psychology, deeper than emotion. It springs up in the innermost place of our being. This joy is of God, and it comes from God, by his loving grace.

Meister Eckhart, a great spiritual teacher and Dominican priest who lived in the late thirteenth and early fourteenth centuries, knew this innermost place well. He knew the joy that comes from God. In a sermon he said,

> ...there is a power in the soul that...flows from the spirit and remains in the spirit and is wholly spiritual. In this power God is always verdant and blossoming in all the joy...that he is in himself. That is a joy so heartfelt, a joy so incomprehensible and great that no one can tell it.[3]

This "power in the soul" is in every person. The joy created there by God is for everyone. Yet no one can force it because it is God's. We can say yes to it; we can open our hearts and our lives to receive it.

This divine joy is always available because God never stops giving. God does not wait until we have done a good deed or until we have become everything we can be. God pours his own joy on all the world, all the time. His grace waits for nothing. It is not a matter of who we are. What counts is who he is. It is God's very nature to give and give and give. Jesus reminds us that God lovingly sends the rain on everyone, good and bad. (See Matthew 5:45.) So also does God's joyfulness flow for everyone. God never withholds any good from us.

Saint Augustine put it beautifully in his *Confessions* to God: "O Lord my God...you are yourself eternal joy, you yourself are joy and those around you find their joy forever in you....And from us you never depart, yet we with difficulty return to you."[4]

His last comment shows that Augustine experienced our human reluctance to go to God completely for this joy.

We know that resistance can be a part of our lives. Joy remains a rare experience for many of us, simply because we do not know how to open ourselves to this depth of grace. We are taught much about enduring suffering. We are taught very little about opening our hearts to a spirit of Christian joy. We may also be sorely wounded. Whatever the cause, our hearts too often remain defensively closed against the gracious joy of God. Sometimes joy may overwhelm us in spite of our defenses. Most of the time, though, we need openness to experience that joy that is, in fact, always at hand.

Doesn't it seem a little strange that we should resist joy, resist peace, and yet we do. We want joy, we want God, but often our ego does not want it. Our miseries are so familiar, our habits of self-protection and hurting and resentment are so strong, that many times we do resist opening ourselves to joy. I have felt myself resisting. If you are active in spiritual growth, you will have noticed your own resistance too.

As Christians we must believe that joy is our birthright. If we do not feel the joy of the Spirit, then the obstacles are in ourselves, never in God. We can trust totally God's generosity, his constant giving. If we are blocked, we can ask him for help to open up our hearts. God always helps. He is already helping, but we simply do not recognize it, nor do we allow it to enter our awareness, our decisions, our living.

One obstacle to joy may be an assumption that spiritual wonders are for heaven, while earth is for pain and other undesirables. In this all-too-common view, we are meant to suffer here and be joyful there. This cannot be so.

The promises of Jesus Christ are for this life as well as a life to come. Surely we cannot read the gospels and believe Jesus meant to say, "Be as miserable as possible now and later you'll get goodies." He promised his followers peace beyond understanding, love fuller than any human love, and joy beyond measure. These were the qualities of his kingdom. He said that this kingdom, the full rule of God in our hearts, is now, here, at hand, within us. (See Luke 10:8-11 and Luke 17:21.)

The human life of Jesus was in this world. The Resurrection means Jesus Christ is for now. His power in our lives is for now. His joy in our hearts is for now. If all his gifts of joyfulness and peace increase in eternity, how wonderful! Let that not distract us from seeking his gifts here on this earth.

In the Christian spiritual life, in the life lived in the inner kingdom, joy is the mark of something happening. It shows that we are beginning to be more open, that we are coming closer to the heart of God. As someone said, "Joy is the flag flying over the castle of the soul, telling us the king is in residence."

Joy is not merely an element of the spiritual journey. Joy is rooted in the Holy Spirit; it is the Spirit's movement within us that causes our hearts to well up full of joy. Once again the work of the Holy Spirit is to transform us into Christ, to make us totally one with him and with the Father. This being so, joy becomes the very atmosphere of the whole transformative process. The transforming work of the Holy Spirit is a joyful work. We are meant to experience that joy for ourselves. Transformation may hurt sometimes, too, but that need never diminish our joy. Indeed, one of the more spectacular events of spiritual growth occurs when we find that inner joy which is not related to pains and displeasures but is beyond them and untouchable.

The Presence of Suffering

All this is not to ignore the presence of suffering in Christian life. All life includes pain; this is part of every human existence. Pain is purposeful and necessary as well as sometimes unnecessary.

Physical pains come and go, emotional pain changes, but pain is part of each human life.

Suffering also comes in the spiritual life. This suffering usually stems from one cause, the ego-centered self. That is the part of myself that says things like "me," "mine," and "keep," and for the most part usually dominates our living. As the life of God grows within us, this ego is gradually restrained and put in its proper place. That place is a servant's place, for this self-concern is important for life in this world. Only it cannot be the ruler of life if we wish God to be our Ruler. The ego does not appreciate being shoved aside from its central position. The ego fights God's growing life in us and that hurts.

We all experience suffering and struggle. Unfortunately, we may not realize that pain does not prevent joy. God's joy is beyond all suffering. This does not mean "when suffering is over, I'll be joyful." God's gracious gift of joy can — and often does — come right in the midst of our pains and our struggles. Joy can become the atmosphere in which we experience pain. It is like this: we live in air, in light. They are our atmosphere. Whether we experience pain or suffering while we are in the air or light does not change the sunshine or the breezes.

Again, Meister Eckhart has wise words for us:

> …when our Lord says: "If any man will come to me, he should deny himself and take up his cross and follow me," it is not merely a command, as people usually say and think. It is a promise and a divine teaching about how all a man's suffering, all his work, all his life can become joyful and happy for him.[5]

Imagine that! Self-denial and taking up the cross are not for the sake of suffering. They are for the sake of joy.

This book is mainly about joy. There is little here about suffering. There seem to be many books, sermons, and workshops available to help us with our pains and our woundedness, and they are valuable. There are reasons for emphasizing the role of suffering in Christian spirituality.

Still, for Lent, let us put aside our suffering (it will be there on its own!) and refrain from concentrating on our pain. Instead, let us ponder the joy of the journey, the ecstasy of the goal. Let us reduce our resistance and open our hearts to the wonder of the joy that Jesus intends for us to experience.

Our very desire for joy is actually planted in our hearts by God. He created us so that our hunger for joy will find fulfillment nowhere else than in himself. An ancient Indian book, the *Upanishads,* says: "There is no joy in the finite, there is joy only in the Infinite." Real and lasting joy comes only as we follow our longing for it and find God. If along the way we also find greater peace, more love, and a more thoroughly Christian life, so much the better!

Initial Lenten Practices

Let us begin with a few simple practices that can give us a swift start.

1. We can pray for joy. We so often pray for everything except what we most deeply want: joy, peace, love. We can ask God to show us his joy, to open our hearts to his joy. It is necessary that we pray not only with words but also with deeds and decisions. If we do, our Lent will become a long, intense prayer for living joy.

2. We can give thanks for joy; we can recall past feelings of joy and give thanks for those moments when God "got through" to us. The giving of thanks for spiritual goodness increases our capacity to receive. Let us take advantage of that and offer gratitude for joys past.

3. We can keep a small log, or journal, each evening writing two "most joyful" items from that day. The days of Lent will give us

numerous memorable moments. Written down, they will be easy to recall and to keep close to our hearts. As we write, we give God thanks for them.

4. To prime our pump for receiving God's joy, we can visualize. Sit down, relax, take a few deep breaths. Quiet yourself for a few minutes. Now recall a joy you have experienced, perhaps even in childhood. Recall images, events — anything that will intensify your awareness of joy in this moment. Savor it. Let the full feeling flow through you. Remain in it for as long as you can. Allow it to take over your being. Wear it as you would a favorite warm sweater or a bright summer shirt.

5. Another quiet exercise is to seek out and discover your innermost feelings. Close your eyes and draw your attention to the space of your heart in your chest. Just attend to it with quiet interest. See what feelings arise. Whatever comes, let it come and let it go. Force nothing. When each feeling passes, seek calmly to go beyond the previous feeling, until you have reached the deepest point you can. It is likely that in this inmost stillness you will feel loving joy or joyful love. Simply stay with it as long as you can. You may also offer this to God. He may intensify it, if you are ready for that. In any case enjoy whatever is given and be grateful for the gift.

Joy is available to us because God always showers it on the hearts of his people. Joy is available to our experience if we become people who look for it, claim it, and become ever more open to it. God calls everyone to discover his joy in the depths of his or her own heart.

Ultimately, it is possible to live in constant unbroken joy. Life with all its peculiarities will continue to go up and down, but joy can remain.

Presently most of us are far from being open enough to experience God's joy all the time. But we can begin, and beginning will lead us to further reflection on joy as we read and experience the pages of this volume.

You might find it helpful to read the following Scripture verses aloud, simply and attentively, several times. You may want to choose a particular one; memorize it, and keep it as a personal theme for a week of Lent or for all of Lent. You may discover that the context of each listed passage also holds a treasure.

John 17:13
John 16:22-24
Luke 2:19
Luke 1:46-47
Galatians 5:22
1 Thessalonians 1:6
Psalm 119:111-112
Psalm 112:1
Isaiah 12:2-3
Isaiah 55:1-3, 12-13
Sirach 2:8-9

CHAPTER 2

Attachment Hampers Joy

I f we explore the writings left us by the great pilgrims of the spirit or if we are fortunate enough to ask someone who walks the path ahead of us, we soon hear that "attachments and aversions" do not support our spiritual growth. They do not open us to God or to God's joy. It is universally recommended by spiritual writers that we learn detachment. Saint Isaiah the Solitary even calls detachment the "first virtue."

At first glance detachment is not an attractive idea. After all, every single one of us learns attachment in infancy. We like and depend on whatever fills our needs and brings us pleasure. We are attached to mother because she is our survival. We are attached to food and to warm blankets. As soon as we are old enough to know what else brings us pleasure and supports our lives, we become quickly attached to those things. In a comic strip, the character Garfield is mentally counting off the tragedies in the world, and then he says, "But the really important thing is that my food bowl is empty."

The same principle applies to aversions, those elements of life we dislike or hate, the many things that frighten or repulse us. Aversions are important to early survival; we need to be repulsed by anything that can harm us. Unpleasant smells, for example, keep us from eating spoiled food. Aversion is attachment in reverse, and it, too, has a natural place in our lives.

So attachment (and its flip side, aversion) is not a sin. It is a natural process, totally human. We all live in varying states of attachment, and we find much wonderful pleasure in those things that support and enhance our lives. As these pleasures are good, we can be deeply grateful for all of them. We rightfully enjoy what is good for us.

Why, then, do we want to attempt to "unlearn" our attachment? Because, if left alone, attachment/aversion grows and grows until there are many things, people, circumstances, without which we think we cannot be happy. As human beings we cling to them, we seek to control our lives so as always to have them, we get very scared or unhappy if we lose them. Attachments constantly increase in number and in their power over our life's experiences.

Once I got a kitten. I already had a houseful of plants, and a friend warned me that the kitten would likely get into the plants. "That's all right," I said, "I'm not attached to the plants." "Then just watch!"

was her reply. "You'll soon be attached to the cat." How right she was, and when the cat had to be given away, it was very difficult.

Attachment is a sticky state. It causes us to cling and to feel dependent. Often binding us down, it limits freedom and inner vision. How can we be joyfully free within if one piece of us is stuck to one thing and another piece to something else, and another...?

Attachment and aversion are like a bottomless pit into which we quickly toss our pleasures and our dislikes, and then we are out looking for more. This attitude of hanging onto certain things in life will never stop of its own accord. It cannot be satisfied by trying to give it all it wants. It will only want more.

Attachment was the problem with the man in Jesus' parable who was so busy building bins for all the things he clung to that he was startled and unprepared when God asked for his soul. (See Luke 12:16-20.) How often we are much like the person in the parable.

As attachment gathers more and builds us, our whole life and personality soon seem *to be* those characteristics, circumstances, possessions, and relationships to which we are deeply attached and those we carefully seek to avoid. This is a mistaken definition of ourselves and *that* is what is wrong with attachment. It can cloud our understanding of who we most deeply and truly are, namely, an image of God on this earth and a temple of the Holy Spirit.

We come to discover lasting joy only as we come to experience God's love in our *real* selves. Only as we know in our own living what it means to be the image of God do we become open enough to live in God's constant joy. As we learn, not in words but in experience, who we really are, joy fills us. When we assume we *are* the sum total of all that we are attached to, we cannot not touch that deeper joy. Attachment limits and restricts; it is simply too grabby to allow a person to experience real joy.

Detachment

So the great-souled saints urge us to practice and learn detachment. Detachment does not mean indifference. It means the ability to be inwardly free from circumstances, to find God in all times and places, deep within our own hearts. Detachment is a serene equanimity of attitude toward everything in one's life. It has even been said that the whole spiritual life is really a progressive detachment from everything, except loving God.

In fact, the desire to know and love God is finally the only motivation that will keep us practicing detachment. The depth of peace and joy that pervades our spiritual life with God is ultimately dependent on putting God in the first place. Yet we cannot do this without practicing detachment. It is a kind of circle, but a glorious one; a circle that has the potential to bring joy and hope.

Detachment does not mean we cannot participate fully in life with great gusto and enjoyment. Actually, the detached person participates more fully and more happily than the rest of us because there is no clinging, no neediness, no constant wanting more. There is freedom from all that. The detached person accepts everything, experiences everything, and allows it all to go its natural way with a blessing. Meister Eckhart told his listeners that to the detached person "all creatures are put to enjoy, for [one] enjoys all creatures in God and God in all creatures."[6] If we ponder what that would actually entail, we will recognize that it is a very high goal.

During Lent we are urged by the Church to some kind of ascetic practice, that is, doing without something we like or undertaking something we do not especially like. From the standpoint of spiritual growth, all ascetic practices, be they tiny or intense, are fundamentally aimed at the lessening of attachment/aversion and the increase of detachment. Growing detachment gives rise to the experience of joyfulness. It is this interior joy that has kept the severe ascetics "at it," and even though we need not starve or beat ourselves, that joy will keep us moving toward God as well.

Detaching ourselves even a little bit opens us to the joy that is already present and waiting for us. In the Introduction, I mentioned a woman at a concert who "tries to distance herself from the situation" by observing herself. The key to her unexpected experience of joy is just this slight "distance" from the situation she did not like. She was attentive, yet not striving for any particular result. She had become a little interested in what was happening, but more as a witness than as an involved participant. She had temporarily quit clinging to her likes and dislikes. Unknown to herself at the time, she attained a small detachment, a small opening. In that uncluttered, momentarily free state, joy flooded into her heart, and everything around her became beautiful.

It is this unclutteredness that is the beginning of detachment. It is not vague. It is interested attention, full recognition of life, but no clinging to anything, no attempting to control anything.

Detachment Is Open and Free

This state of detachment is an open free state. It may last only a moment or it may eventually become one of the foundation stones that supports a spiritual life. The important possibility is that we can know God from this stance. In detachment we can receive and give love very powerfully. We can accept divine gifts, most especially joy. God can give us what he wants us to have. He can communicate himself to us because we are detached enough to be open to him. We can be open to him only to the extent that we are free from clinging to others. That means only to the extent that we are detached in our living. A single experience of the joy that comes with the loosening of attachment is enough to keep us practicing a long time.

This is the deeper reason (though it is rarely said) for the Church's invitation to practice asceticism or holiness during Lent. We learn to be a little more detached, and therefore we can know God a little more closely. Unfortunately, the reasons are not always explained; we are not always told what asceticism is for. We often have the feeling that we are just supposed to hurt and struggle for a while (as if we didn't hurt and struggle enough already).

When we practice some asceticism, we need to remember that our attitude makes all the difference. If we practice detachment with gritted teeth, counting the days until we can again hug our individual coffee pot — well, we are not really practicing perfect detachment, are we? We are doing a nasty task that should be over before long. This is only aversion, that is, the negative form of attachment.

But if we practice generously, with a sense of adventure and experiment, eager to break through our own forms of sticky living, we will find a way. Then joyful peace will increase within us.

How, then, can we make this Lent a lasting contribution toward a life less pervaded by attachments and aversions?

Identifying Attachments and Aversions

First, we need to identify some of our attachments and aversions so we have clear material for practice. Once, years ago, I was with a group who was trying to discover its biggest attachments. I tried to imagine what would be most painful to give away. What was I most attached to? My electric blanket! That told me a lot about the importance I placed on bodily comforts, a whole range of attachments.

By pondering the following questions, you may find some of your attachments and aversions. These questions will help in the process of discovery if you let yourself dwell on the feelings they arouse.

1. What or whom must I have to feel happy?
2. What kinds of possessions do I seek and try to keep? (Don't overlook the obvious, like a place to live.)
3. How do I define myself? Who am I? (Married, a dentist, wearing a certain uniform, holding a certain position, and so on.)
4. Is there something that, if I had it, would make me a different person? Is there something I have, the loss of which would make me a different person?
5. What habits of thought do I cling to? (Opinions, reactions of liking or disliking, old conditioning, hurts, memories.)

Questions like these are tools to help us notice our own state of attachment. The objects to which we are attached do not matter so much, but the intensity of the feeling with which we cling to them has much to do with our living.

Practices

Once we recognize that feeling, we can begin a practice or two that may loosen us up a little. Here are a few suggestions.

1. Find a quiet, relaxed time when you can ponder. Then choose one of your "favorite" objects of attachment. Let it come fully into your awareness. Do not try to evaluate anything. Your purpose here is to get acquainted with "how you are." See it. Feel it. Examine your reactions. Stare at this part of yourself awhile.

Now ask yourself how important this object is
- to your personal identity,
- to your love of God,
- to your joyfulness in living.

If you find that even those objects that you think you need are less important than you have assumed, is it possible that the feeling of attachment itself is also less important?

2. During this Lent do without one thing daily that you want: the morning cup of coffee, the parking place nearest the office (or store), the music you like best, whatever. It need not be the same thing for the whole season.

The point here is not necessarily to "give up something for Lent" but to loosen your tendency to cling to things, people, circumstances. Notice what happens when you do this. Do you feel a touch of new power over yourself? Do you perhaps find resistance? Is there a kind of playfulness or delight? Is the experiment itself pleasurable? Do you feel more open in the moment that you let go of your favorite objects of attachment?

3. The reverse of number two is to do something daily that you normally do not like, and do it freely without any resentment or resistance. Again, you may choose something different each day. Again, try to observe your reactions as just described.

4. Every day during Lent, when you feel troubled or irritated or worried, remember to say to yourself, "It doesn't matter." (I do not refer to catastrophes; these are too big for this practice now.) You may feel quite strange, as if you were lying to yourself. Do not be concerned about that. Just repeat it. "It doesn't matter." Give yourself a chance to see that, more than likely, it really doesn't matter, and certainly not as much as your reaction would suggest.

Once I had just explained this practice to a monastic community on retreat. Then I discovered that I had failed to bring enough handout sheets for everyone. My frustration was obvious for all to see. There was a chorus of "it doesn't matter!" Then we all had a good laugh — and it truly didn't matter — and I was free of it. It was not that terribly important.

This simple practice may also result in a renewed ability to laugh at yourself, to take many things more lightly. That, too, is detachment and is to be honored. With a lighter attitude, joy finds many more little alleyways into our daily awareness.

5. During this Lent, whenever you notice that you are expressing an opinion to yourself or others, pause. "I think..." is the tip-off to another kind of attachment. We "think" many things that clutter our hearts. So when we pause to notice our opinions, and our clinging to them, we can also practice saying, "It seems to me" or "I don't really know." We can even practice saying nothing at all on the subject.

We thus practice detachment from our own opinions and concepts. After all, how many times in our lives have we "changed our minds"? Opinions come and go like the wind. We can be free of them. Then we can see life as it truly is, full of the love of God, full of his grace and his joy, regardless of our opinions.

6. Probably the most powerful practice of detachment is this: to attempt to let go of the results of our actions. Usually, we plan our actions according to what we hope will be a certain expected result. But we can act according to our love of God or our experimenting in Lent or our desire for true joy. Our actions are our responsibility but, in fact, the results are not ours; they are God's. So we can practice doing what we need to do and then letting go of any thought of result or reward, giving that to God.

It is wonderful to be free of clinging to results, free of "controlling interests" in life's events and one's own behavior. This freedom opens one's heart wide. The joy that attends this freedom is not easily described, but it is most worthy of our practice. Try it! Then try it again.

Finally, as we practice detachment, let us do it playfully. It is not a game exactly, since we are moving toward the most profound goal in human life: union with God. But when we get too solemn about our efforts or too sticky in our piety, we close ourselves off from grace by a subtle selfishness. Let's try to sport a little at this practice. The lightness itself is akin to joy. The gospel constantly begs us to be joyful.

Then we may look forward to the day when we can say with

Symeon, the New Theologian: "Happy is he who passionately embraces you, for he will be wondrously changed! In spirit and in soul he will rejoice, because you are the ineffable joy. Happy is he who gains possession of you, for he will count the treasures of this world as nothing, for you are indeed the truly inexhaustible riches."[7]

Here are Scripture references for your reflection.
Ecclesiastes 2:24-26; 6:7-9 (Actually the whole book is about detachment.)
Matthew 6:31-33
1 Corinthians 7:29-31
2 Corinthians 4:16-18
Galatians 5:16-25
James 4:1-4

CHAPTER 3

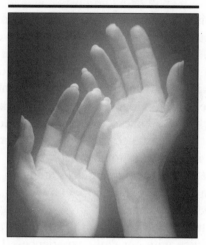

Surrender Opens
the Heart

I n the movies surrender usually means defeat, followed by being
made to do what one does not want to do. The hero never
surrenders; the villains are forced to surrender. Our society seems
convinced that surrender is not for the strong.

Most individuals approach Lent with this feeling. During Lent
we plan *to be* strong and *to do* something. We are going to deny
ourselves or do penance or discipline ourselves. Perhaps we are

going to form a new habit. Maybe we will control ourselves more.

Actually, this is one approach to living. When we are uncomfortable, we resist the discomfort and set ourselves to change the circumstances. We assume that if the circumstances were different, our discomfort would disappear. In our efforts to control our lives, we are often like my grandmother, of whom a member of the family once said, "She goes at things as if she were killing snakes!"

In our search for happiness, even our desire for God, we may not realize that our resistance itself, our penchant to "do" and to change things, is not always totally helpful.

During Lent we are giving particular attention to practices that cooperate with the Holy Spirit in our own transformation. *Surrender* is a rather direct practice of this inner cooperation; it lessens our resistance to God and opens our hearts to his action.

We will practice with our daily experiences. They may not be important in themselves, but they are chances to practice the "how-to" of surrender, of self-giving to God. Meister Eckhart says, "...surrender yourself wholly to God in all things, and then do not trouble yourself about what he may do with his own."[8]

Most of us probably would agree that we want to give ourselves wholly to God. There is within every human heart a center that longs only for this total gift of self to God. As human beings, many of us have lost sight of this deep longing. But even when we feel it, there are many parts of ourselves that do not agree at all. When we are honest, we already know it is not enough to say, "Yes, Lord, I'm yours," because the very next thing we do can easily be in another spirit altogether. Who has not finished with a period of fervent prayer and gone immediately to being critical or resentful?

This division in life is our reason for the practice of surrender. We learn surrender gradually; God supports our efforts until we are more able to give ourselves to him. By Easter our cooperation with God will be a little fuller than it was before Lent began.

Surrender Is Not Weakness

First, let us note that surrender is not weakness because in truth only the strong are able fully to surrender. It is not helplessness; it is not inwardly turning into mush. Surrender is not being taken prisoner of war. It is rather like being a voluntary prisoner of love, to God, and this prison brings us the unusual gift of total freedom.

There is a part in each of us that does not want to surrender to God. We are so sure how the world (or church or home or friend or spouse or child) should be, and we do not want to let go of these concepts. We know how we ourselves should be and how life should proceed. We want to alter circumstances to fit our own ideas, hopes, and dreams. We also hold tightly to old habits, to the ways we learned as a child about how we should live. We like the familiar, the controllable, the safe. We want our lives to be the way we want it.

The actual results of this kind of thinking are not always joyful. Our own way is, in fact, far more narrow than God's way. God has more options for us than we can ever imagine. If we close ourselves toward new life experiences, then we run the risk of closing ourselves to joy. Believing that we know how it all should go leads to negative experiences. We feel angry and impatient and critical; we reject people who do not "fit the right picture"; we feel sad when something goes awry; we get bored because our own way gets monotonous. It requires a certain humility to surrender to another possibility, and humility is built by the practice of surrender.

Surrender Means Yielding

Surrender is a humble yielding of oneself. One of the most effective ways I was ever given to practice yielding happened when I was struck down with pneumonia. I was so weak that there was no question of doing anything except taking my medicine, coughing, and lying there. I did not even have energy to resent the sickness! I was only able, willy-nilly, to yield.

The fruits of that experience are too many to tell: insights, healing of old wounds, patience, increased strength. And there was joy. There I was, horizontal for weeks, and joyfulness without any apparent stimulus wove itself through the whole experience, flowing in and out of my awareness. Since I could only yield to the actual circumstances, a disproportionate intensity of joy was given in return. It could only have been God's gift.

Because we experience our resistance as part of ourselves, surrender may feel like sacrificing what I want in favor of something I don't want. Surrender is a sacrifice, but it sacrifices what I actually do not want (negative experiences) in favor of what I do want (joy, peace, love). Surrender sacrifices our selfishness so God can take it, make it holy, and return it to us — transformed in joy.

As we practice letting go, it helps to remember that the goal is positive. Surrender to God is surrender to Easter, to transformation, to total loving, to fullness of joy. Also, especially as we begin, we need to be aware that our *feelings* will be reeducated as our practice continues and we discover the excellent results of surrender. What we sacrifice is never as great as what we receive when the giver is God.

Surrender can also be viewed as the practice of humble obedience. We have all felt that if only an angel would command us, we would surely obey. But God does not usually work that way. God does provide circumstances that might be considered as assignments. We are called to obey him through *this* situation. In our obeying we learn what he wants us to learn and receive the gift he wants to give us. Thus, surrender is a very practical way of conforming our own will to the will of God in the daily happenings of life.

Each day most certainly brings good moments and bad moments. Surrender and acceptance can be considered as obedience to God himself. It may not seem at all dramatic. It may be quite ordinary, like burnt breakfast toast. But an accumulation of small surrenders can change us deeply. One of these changes will certainly be an increase of humility, for true surrender requires humility as we face life's realities. Our hearts are opened so that we gradually can allow our lives to be led by his guiding hand. We begin to receive God's gracious love and joy directly.

As with all of these Lenten practices, our attitude is vital. If we begrudge our surrender, we are kidding ourselves, are we not? So we try to surrender willingly, trustfully. As our heart opens to be generous to this one little situation, it opens wider for God. It also helps to be experimental with our practice, to stay light. If we mentally turn these practices into a moral demand, something will be lost. That something eventually is joy. Practices undertaken with a measure of free generosity (or even just willingness to see what will happen) soon expand into joy of themselves.

The Practice of Surrender

Surrender has three elements. When we surrender we let go of our unreasonable resistance. We stop digging in with our emotional heels. Second, we allow our immediate situation to be exactly as it is without violent emotional reaction (or, if emotions come, we allow them until they have altered themselves). We simply let it all be. Third, we give ourselves inwardly and actively with a generous heart to that to which we have surrendered.

Here is an example:

Recently my husband asked me to take a day off with him and go to the mountains. I felt the rush of immediate resistance. I was heavily involved in a project that I wanted to continue. I usually enjoy being outdoors with my husband, but not this day, not this time. At the same time I knew he needed the day off. What happened was simple; I had decided to go, but the decision was not clean.

There was still a great deal of internal resistance that I did not see. Every suggestion he made I did not like: I did not want to picnic, I did not want to hike, I did not want him to take photos, and I kept on not liking whatever came up until my unreasonableness became apparent even to me. Finally, I paused and thought, "What a good opportunity to practice surrender."

First, give up resisting. It is quite possible to quit fighting, even if we have to quit several times before it sticks. This was a minor issue, so I just quit. Second, as we got into the car to go to the mountains, I allowed the circumstances to be: here we are, and here is where I'll be for quite a while, so that's how it is. I'm going to be out all day. Third, how can I give myself generously to this jaunt? I let myself appreciate the scenery. I reminded myself of how much I love my husband. I thanked God for safety on the road and for the beauty of the hills. Soon the surrender was complete, laughter came easily, and joy came around to greet me.

Exercises

Here are several exercises. Or you may take the three steps just given and invent your own exercises.

1. Each day be alert to moments of irritation or frustration. These can be traffic, people, computers down, something lost, disappointment, unwelcome duties, physical pain — anything we quite naturally tend to resist.

When you notice such a moment, pause. Quiet yourself inside and attempt to stop resisting. Whatever it is — body, mind, emotions — notice it clearly. Let it be. Remain as still within as you can and feel the feelings. Just allow it to be whatever it is. If you can induce a little tenderness into your awareness, so much the better.

Then watch what happens next. Usually, we discover that the present moment, as it actually is, is not as bad as our reaction. Our reaction consists of past associations and future expectations, but the present by itself is quite livable.

2. In a quiet place, relax. Ask God to guide your exercise. Think of your relationship with a person or a situation that should be changed. You know how it should be, so let all your feelings surface into awareness. Really get into it, both mentally and emotionally. Notice all your ideas, plans, and determinations around this person or circumstance. Does this bundle of thoughts and feelings leave room for joy?

Now gently allow all your reactions to flow quietly away. Maybe you do not know how it really should be. Let it go. Maybe it does not matter as much as you thought. Let it go. See all of it flow away. Notice the present moment again, gently. What is it like to let go of all these conceptions?

3. Again, in a leisurely way, acknowledge God as your partner in Lenten practice. Then call to mind something in your own life from which you would like to be free. It may be a pain, a habit, an emotional reaction, something you could call a "negativity."

Try to give this undesired presence your full attention. See how much it actually is inside you. Then acknowledge that it is there. You need not approve nor disapprove. Simply, quietly, give it an assent. For a moment give it permission to be there.

Now turn to God. Give this undesired presence to him, without any self-scolding. "This is in me, God. I give it to you now, to change or not to change. I do not want it any longer. Please accept it." Surrender to the negativity first; then surrender the negativity to God. It may not suddenly disappear. You may not experience anything at first. But over time something will happen because you have let go of something for God to transform.

4. Try giving yourself very generously to a situation you do not like. One man worked years at a job he disliked. He decided the best surrender would be always to do his best, no matter what. Another person in her work was repeatedly assigned mindless

tasks. She gave herself to them by repeating the "Jesus Prayer" as a constant background. Try to find your own way, but stay with it in a free and open spirit.

The ultimate goal of the practice of surrender is to make surrender to God a constant companion of one's spiritual life. Along the way we will more than likely experience many side benefits. One of them may be an increase in energy. We normally spend a lot of energy in resistance. As we gradually stop resisting, we have that energy available for other pursuits. If we use that energy toward loving God, the joy will be doubled.

Another side benefit is that life seems easier. It has often happened that people's circumstances change very little after they begin to practice surrender: their physical sickness remains; they still must do the nasty job; the people around them are the same. But — here is the surprise — everything *seems* different because they are no longer fighting. They discover that at least half our pain is made of our personal resistance to pain. When we surrender, half the pain disappears, so life seems to have improved greatly.

When we surrender to our lives as they are, our lives will change of themselves. As we surrender to God, the Spirit changes us from inside out. So let us try to practice surrendering during Lent, whatever it may include. Then we will be much more able to surrender to the joys of our own Easter.

It should be observed that the whole idea of surrender does not include surrendering principles. If a person wishes us to steal or to harm another, we cannot surrender obviously. This entire concept is understood to mean that we surrender unreasonable resistance.

Here are Scripture references for your reflection.
Proverbs 3:5-6
Psalm 32:8-9
Psalm 55:23
1 Samuel 15:22

Ecclesiastes 3:1-15
Psalm 84:12-13
Psalm 125:1-2; 126:5-6
Matthew 6:34
2 Corinthians 6:4-10; 12:10
Philippians 2:8

CHAPTER 4

Contentment: Finding Delight Everywhere

An ancient Indian story tells of a great saint who put this question to her followers. "Which person," she asked, "is happier: one with ten children or one with ten million dollars?"

The followers pondered the advantages and disadvantages of each situation but could not answer their teacher.

She finally said, "The one with ten children — because he *knows* he doesn't want any more!" Obviously, this levity has a purpose as we begin these comments on contentment.

Contentment with what is — in our lives — provides a strong foundation for real happiness. We often feel that contentment is an involuntary experience that comes when we have everything we want. But that is a misconception for two reasons. One is that, in fact, we never have "everything we want." Desires multiply themselves without end if we let them. The other reason is that contentment is, in its beginnings, a voluntary state of mind. At its most profound, contentment is a high spiritual state, a gift of God to our spirit. It is the deepest peace of heart. We can receive it only if we have practiced it long enough to make an interior place for it.

Contentment is never just a matter of a full stomach or a soft bed or any external circumstance. Contentment originates within ourselves. Contentment is a fundamental satisfaction with our lives as they are, a quiet, steady acceptance even in the midst of constant changes. This sense of "okay-ness" about life gives us relief from striving toward the future or pushing toward new circumstances. If we are contented, we can freely relax, smile, and appreciate our lives.

Contentment is even more; it is the capacity to welcome whatever comes unsought. It is as if we are enabled to say a warm "hello" to each person, each situation, or each event that comes into our lives. All religious traditions seem to possess stories about contentment because it is not a common virtue. Here is an example said to have come from India.

An ascetic was sitting quietly under a tree. A man came and brought him a blanket, left it, and went away. The ascetic nodded and smiled. The ascetic looked at the blanket awhile, then was about to wrap it around his shoulders when a beggar came along and took it for himself. The ascetic nodded and smiled. Soon a woman came with a bowl of steaming rice and left it for him. He nodded and smiled. He paused to give thanks and in that pause another beggar came and took the rice away. The ascetic nodded and smiled.

In all our lives all things come to us and all things leave us. It is the nature of life on earth. We often are more ready to grab them than we are to smile, nod, and appreciate. If we are contented, we welcome each circumstance as it comes, not only those we happen to find pleasing.

Contentment is not the same as resignation, at least not as we usually understand resignation. The resigned person feels, "Well, these are the circumstances and I can't do much about them, so I'll resign myself to them and go on." There is nothing wrong with this; it is simply not enough. In contrast, the contented person says, "Wow! I certainly didn't expect this, but let me see what delight I can find in it." Contentment takes delight in life as it actually is.

Contentment is also not complacency, with oneself or one's life or one's world. True contentment creates so much positive experience that one is already different from the discontented. It creates a climate where change, when needed or when it comes of itself, is welcomed. It allows one to move toward growth peaceably and without force. Since contentment neither grasps at situations nor demands particular results, it frees God to act in a person's life without hindrance.

Contentment is essentially, then, a quiet, open stance in the heart and mind, a delight in what is, and a willingness to be led by God's circumstances.

Contentment in This World

How about contentment in this world that seems to have so much wrong with it? Can a contented person change the world? The answer is yes, and more powerfully than a discontented one. First, a contented person spreads peace in all human contacts, while a striving, uneasy person fills the atmosphere with negative feelings.

The very existence of a contented person means that a corner of the world is a more peaceful place.

Moreover, each person is called by God to some service to the world. If each of us obeys this call, however small or large it may seem, God will do in the world what he wants done through us. Again, contentment serves this possibility because it frees us from all our "what-about-me?" worries. We are then more able to follow our God-given calling.

We may never change the world in big ways. Even so, our responsibility is to serve as he calls us, with contentment in our heart. The joy in this approach to life is astounding! Service of all kinds is joy-giving, but the service of a contented heart and mind opens to the river of joy that is God's grace.

Habits Eroding Contentment

A number of human habits erode the possibility of contentment. Their opposites are tools for the practice of contentment.

One is the frequently heard, "If only...." If only I hadn't done that, if only my parents..., if only the Church..., if only my neighbors would — *then* I would be content. "If only" betrays a discontented heart. In a person possessing this comment, contentment simply does not arise. The opposite of "if only" is simple acceptance and acknowledgment of the facts as they are.

Another habit is comparison of ourself (life, circumstances) with those of another. "I wish I were like that!" "Why don't I have that thing (quality, event, object) in my life?" And worst of all, "I want what you have." This is envy. There is a reason for it to be forbidden by one of the Ten Commandments (Exodus 20:17). Envy destroys one's own peace; it makes contentment impossible. It leads to self-pity, which is the total opposite of contentment and perhaps the worst thing we can do to ourselves. Further, envy destroys human relationships. How can I be a friend if I want what you have?

The antidote for envious comparison is twofold: stop comparing is likely the best method. If you find yourself doing so, choose to rejoice that the thing (quality, position, and so on) you envy is doing its good work in the world. Be glad of its existence.

Complaining is another habit that is a symptom of discontentment. Walter Hilton, a great English mystic, says, "The more you grumble...the less is the image of Jesus Christ reformed in you."[9] The best way out of this is just don't do it. Don't do it mentally or vocally. Give your mind something else to do every time you begin to complain. Distract your own attention to a better use of your mind.

Unbridled, uncontrolled ambition destroys contentment too. A whole chapter could be written on the effects of ambition. Like any unwelcome desire, it can grow to take over one's entire life. The wrong kind of ambition is often totally selfish. The antidote for ambition is finding pleasure in each moment as it comes along. The selfish desire to be more, bigger, better, needs to be given to God for purification. Then each moment becomes a gift to be enjoyed. Soon contentment enters the heart.

Restlessness and boredom are also enemies of contentment. These are epidemic habits in our society because our ordinary lives are so "hyper." We are overstimulated constantly. There is always sound; at every hour of the night, cities roar. There are always lights; places to go and things to do multiply so fast. If we come upon moments without stimulation, we simply do not know what to do with ourselves, so we fret restlessly. We feel bored until we can go at it again.

One person who wanted contentment took to welcoming his boredom, watching it, investigating it, finding out how it worked inside himself. Soon, of course, it disappeared because he became so interested in his observations! Even more useful would be a daily time for complete wakeful relaxation without any stimulations.

Key to Contentment

With all these familiar responses beckoning our attention, how can we be contented?

Saint Paul gives us a key. In his letter to the Christian community of Philippi, he says he is content in all circumstances because "...I have learned, in whatever situation I find myself, to be self-sufficient" (Philippians 4:11). The circumstances of his life, you will remember, were often extreme and required great strength. For the strength he needed, for his contentment, he turned to God.

We need to turn to God and cooperate with his desire that we be filled with contentment. One method to be used is to seek in all situations the gift God has placed there for us. If we are practicing so as to cooperate with the Holy Spirit (our aim for Lent), then the Spirit provides circumstances through which we can receive what we need. Nothing comes to us which holds no gift. We can practice being willing to look deeply enough to find it.

Once we realize this, every new circumstance is like a surprise package. We can trust in the loving hand of God who gives it to us. For our growth into Christ, God gives at every moment what is best for us, for our growth, for our healing. If we ignore or resist what he gives, in whatever wrapping he gives it, do we not throw away the very thing we most desire, which is a close relationship with God?

But if we take delight in each event as it comes, seeking there what God will show us, then his presence becomes almost palpable. We become more and more open. Joy begins to bubble up within us again.

Some years ago in a thirty-day retreat, Father Armand Nigro read a poem to us, the gist of which was this. A woman found her life deeply burdensome, and she cried out to the Lord. She had complaints (justifiable, of course) and she had questions and she wanted changes in her life. Finally, after many days of appeal, the

Lord appeared to her. She was astonished indeed. He said, "My daughter, I have come to respond to all your complaints and your questions. Would you say them to me one at a time?" She started to answer, but all her desires had disappeared. Finally, she said to the Lord, "Well, now that you are here, there seems to be nothing I need."

The Lord is always here. We forget this, do we not? We do not pay attention to our hearts where he is always present, so we think he is absent. In the end we can be contented only insofar as we are centered on God and know his presence in all things. Then permanent contentment will arise in us as his gift.

When we practice contentment, we become more aware of the Lord's presence. When we are aware of the Lord's presence, contentment becomes our joy.

As a prelude to a few practices for contentment, here are questions to ponder:
1. Do I actually believe circumstances or people must change in order for me to feel contented?
2. Do I like a peaceful, contented attitude, or do I actually prefer being stirred up? (This is tricky; please be honest.)
3. In what ways each day can I look for delight in things as they are?

Practices

Here are exercises for practice during this Lent. The first one could be done weekly. The others could even become daily habits so they become a constant in our living.

1. Become quiet and relaxed. Recall a time when you involuntarily felt completely contented, when everything was okay and even better than okay. Recall the feelings you had then. Let that feeling come to you now. Let it expand and fill your whole awareness. Revel in the beauty of that contented feeling.

Now, staying in touch with that feeling, become aware of this present moment and all it contains. Let your feeling of contentment flow from your heart into all aspects of this moment: yourself, your surroundings, your family, work, friends. Be utterly contented in your heart. Give thanks to God for this moment of contentment. Ask him to increase it.

2. Practice gratitude. Give thanks for everything, no matter how small or how difficult. Say with each new event, "Thank you, God, for giving me this moment's gift." Practice this many times each day.

3. Stop what you are doing. Say to yourself, "I have everything I need. God generously supplies all my needs." Repeat this over and over for several minutes. Notice how you feel, what happens inside. If you like, turn it into prayer.

As a practice, this may feel strange at first, especially if you are usually not very contented. Be persistent. Try to remember that contentment is an attitude, not an external fact. We use this true statement to correct an attitude. So even if it feels foreign to you, make an attempt to practice it.

4. Turn back to the beginning of this chapter where the enemies of contentment are discussed. Choose the one that is most familiar to you and begin to practice its opposite as given there.

Here are Scripture references for your reflection.
Psalm 8
Psalm 40:9
Psalm 92:2-5
Sirach 29:23; 30:15-16
2 Corinthians 12:10
Hebrews 13:5
1 Timothy 6:6-11

CHAPTER 5

The Practice of Noninjury

One of the most fascinating experiments in being open to a spirit of joy is the practice of noninjury. The idea is simple. Noninjury is the effort to do no harm to any being by act, word, or thought. Today the term noninjury is more common in Eastern religious devotion than in Western Christianity. Jesus urged it, however, when he said, "Blessed are the meek, for they will inherit the land" (Matthew 5:5).

45

Meekness has acquired a false meaning. It is often assumed that the meek are the weak; they are life's doormats who cannot do anything better than lie down and take it.

Meekness actually is a way of walking on the earth so that a person attempts to leave no hurtful mark on any of the inhabitants. Meekness tries to live in respect for all, affection for all, and reverence for all. Meekness is fundamental nonviolence; it is life in harmony with everything.

Noninjury is meekness. Anyone who has tried knows that affection and reverence cannot be produced by mere decision. Noninjury as a practice is so immediately possible; in fact, it can be a wonderful door to the deeper possibilities of joy in God.

What are the elements of the practice of noninjury? First, harmlessness needs to extend to all: to people, to animals, to plants, to inanimate objects, and to oneself, and even to the atmosphere that we share. Most of us easily see the outward value of not injuring other people (except, of course, if we think there is good reason). We also are taught to be kind to animals, unless we need them for food or for science. We are not so concerned about plants, as they are assumed to be unconscious anyway. Inanimate objects need no particular regard from us. What difference can it make to a machine whether we respect it or not?

Notice that in such thoughts our focus is outward, on the object, rather than inward, in our own hearts. But in regard to this somewhat new idea of noninjury, like all spiritual practices, it is undertaken primarily for our interior growth. For inner peace it makes little difference whether our fist strikes a face or a door, whether we yell at a computer or a person. The inner unrest is the same; it may prevent us from receiving the joy of God's own life.

So we may practice noninjury as an excellent Lenten effort: it changes us permanently, from the inside out. It cooperates strongly with the transformative work of the Holy Spirit.

Inflicting No Harm

Let us begin. Let us try, for one day, to do no harm to anything.

For this we must look first of all to our actions. Rarely do most of us become physically violent toward other people, yet some of us do. Those few can begin their experiment in noninjury at this most obvious point of harmfulness and resolve not to be violent toward other people.

We can look further. Do we do physical damage to anything? Have we kicked the cat lately? Have we thrown something in anger and frustration? Have we slammed a door? If we wish to practice noninjury here, our first possibility is, when possible, to apologize to the things we perhaps have hurt. "To a door?" Yes, to a door. The point, remember, is not the door; it is our own heart. And yes, we may feel quite silly. But try it (maybe silently!) and watch what happens inside, feel what happens inside. We can also do the opposite and express our gratitude to animals and plants who have become food for us: their life is sacrificed for ours. Thank them! Be light about it. Experiment. And for goodness' sake, don't take this all too severely. We are learning to be filled with joy.

A Benedictine nun tells this story on herself. She was in a Zen Buddhist monastery helping in the office. The copier was producing terrible copies, and she was getting more and more frustrated with the thing. Nasty words came from her mouth (and heart!), and finally she smacked the copier a good one with her hand.

The house superior was watching. He told her that maybe her personal attitude was causing the problem. Being a good Westerner, knowledgeable about machines, she did not believe him. He took the original paper from her and placed it in the machine. He put his palms together and bowed to the copier, then pushed the button and, of course, got a splendid copy. "Coincidence!" her mind shouted. Perhaps. But *his peace was not disturbed;* hers had long ago fled.

This story pushed me into extending my kindness to my own computer, which I had never liked. I removed a clever but hostile cartoon that I had taped on the monitor. Has the computer behaved better? I don't really know, but I do know that layers of resistance to my work have slid away from my heart. I enjoy my work much more and find the days lighter and easier to handle.

As we stop stepping on ants, yanking on knotted yarn, pounding on tables, something many times happens inside us. We attend better to ourselves; we notice when we are not at peace or when we are inwardly closed. This is important, because we can change in ourselves only what we know is there.

Another level of noninjury occurs in regard to our speech. Rare are those who have never hurt anyone with words, either deliberately or unaware. The practice of noninjury requires that we give more attention to our words; we begin to think before we speak. Obviously, this requires considerable self-restraint, even though it sounds deceptively simple. The mind understands the idea, but the egocentric part of us does not necessarily cooperate.

A great saint has said that noninjury in speech means running a triple check on any words before we say them, asking these questions: Are they true? Are they necessary? Are they kind?

If we were to practice this check, for at least some individuals, a large proportion of conversation would be silenced. Still, the words we could say would be lovely and add beauty to any relationship, to any workplace, to any circumstance.

Even subtler is the practice of noninjury in thought. Criticism, complaint, dogmatic opinions, self-pity — all these and all their cousins are targeted here. If I had spoken every critical thought I've ever had, I would have dealt far more injury to others. As it was, I injured mostly (though hardly exclusively) myself.

We humans are prone to be judgmental and intolerant in thought, even when we do not express it in words. In noninjury we practice letting go of these thoughts and replacing them with something kinder. Even in thought we practice being the meek of the earth.

Refusing to harm does not mean that we allow others to harm us. When one allows the hurtful acts or words of others to go unchallenged, one contributes to the sum total of violence in the world. A person who acts harmfully is out of control and needs help to stop. The practicer of noninjury must find ways to limit that hurtfulness.

Moreover, allowing harm to oneself is *doing* harm to oneself, and the practice of noninjury must include not hurting oneself. A noninjurious life respects all God's creation, including oneself. To do no injury to oneself implies allowing no injury to be done to us, insofar as we can prevent it.

This is not easy. To learn to set definite limits on the hurtful behavior of others, without harming in return, we must think and work and pray for it. We must deeply desire to become truly harmless.

When we look more closely at our own treatment of ourselves, we usually find that we are astoundingly harsh with ourselves. Stephen Levine, in *Healing Into Life and Death,* shows again and again how unkindly we respond to our own life, our own being. For example, how do we react when we accidentally hurt ourselves physically? As human beings we might react with emotional violence, resistance, and harsh words.

Once a washing machine lid fell on my fingertip, and the shock was terrific. A moment after my violent expletive, I remembered Levine's words and tried hard to focus respectfully on the finger and not resist the pain. It took all the will power I had. Did it change the finger? I have no idea, but it did demonstrate clearly the difference in my feelings when I am kinder to myself. At least I tried to adjust what is a normal behavior pattern.

We are unkind to ourselves in mental chatter. A lot of mean thoughts might fill our minds. For example, "Marilyn, you are so dumb! Why did you do such a stupid thing?" We try not to speak this way to friends; be nice to yourself as well.

We also often act harmfully to ourselves. We at times over-indulge in food or in other harmful habits that might injure our bodies. We do not act as kindly as we could in caring for ourselves. Do we exercise? Do we play? Do we often drive ourselves harder than we would ever drive a friend? Let's try to stop hurting ourselves; our practice of noninjury can begin here.

Results of Practicing Noninjury

What results can we anticipate as we practice noninjury?

Jesus said, "The measure with which you measure will in return be measured out to you" (Luke 6:38). Saint Paul reminds the Galatians, "A person will reap only what he sows" (Galatians 6:7). The resolve to do no injury calls forth gentleness within us. We will discover that gentleness will begin to flow back to us. As we become truly kindly, the world of our experience will become more kindly, and we will enjoy it more.

Our habitual internal attitude also pervades our prayer. If we are violent inside, we may find deeper prayer impossible or, at the least, extremely difficult. We will be unable to become quiet enough to receive God's responses. When we want to be quiet and pray, our inner turmoil may threaten to overwhelm us. Contemplative prayer will be out of reach until we are less injurious in our attitudes. Meekness helps develop a contemplative attitude in our heart.

As we practice, we may experience a gradually increasing easiness toward our everyday life. We will be calmer, more patient, more loving, and probably more humorous. As we try to restrain ourselves from harming, our tolerance will increase. As we become more interested in preserving our inner equilibrium, unwelcome circumstances become opportunities to practice some of these new attitudes. With that, we are no longer emotionally tossed about so much. Our inner life becomes more harmonious and peaceful, more tranquil and joyous.

In time noninjury changes our attitude toward all of living. As we cease harming others, we become more open to ourselves. We grasp less and accept more. We demand less and appreciate more. We become more free as we realize what our *needs* really are. We discover that often the only barriers to our happiness have been our own violent attitudes and our own pushy habits. Most precious of all, the grace of God — that is joy — will enter our lives more and more frequently.

We may feel a growing kinship with everything. When I touch something gently, with reverence in my heart, it becomes a co-creature with me. We discover anew, as the Buddha said, that "all beings love life" and they all deserve our care. Here is a basis for ecological effort. Widespread practice of noninjury to the earth would bring the necessary revolution in our living to allow nature to heal herself.

The story is told of Abba Bes, one of the early Desert Fathers, who was renowned for his complete meekness, since he never spoke harshly and lived in complete serenity. There was a wild hippopotamus rampaging in the neighborhood, so they called Abba Bes to help. He allowed the raging beast to come near him, then said gently, "In the name of Jesus Christ, I order you not to ravage this countryside anymore." The beast was not seen in that area again. Was this a miracle? Only insofar as meekness in a human being is miraculous.

Awhile after I began practicing noninjury, my husband and I went camping. We love to sit at a little distance and watch the animals live. One day while praying, a squirrel started watching me as I was watching him. He suddenly hopped over in my direction. I did not move a muscle as he came, hoping he would come closer. He paused, looked me full in the eye, and then proceeded confidently and placed his front paws on my bare foot. He stayed there a whole minute. Was the creature begging? Perhaps. But my heart rejoiced at this sign of acceptance by a wild thing, and it seemed to acknowledge that I had become more akin to creation. Jesus said the meek will inherit the land, the earth. What if he meant it quite literally, as well as figuratively?

With continued practice, everything will seem richer. By wishing not to hurt, I allow all things to be. Then I see more clearly and appreciate more fully each thing, each person in his or her own unique identity and function. Strangers slowly disappear into kinship. The beauty in every simple thing becomes apparent.

As such changes occur in us, we gradually experience a certain sacredness in everything. Little by little we notice that things bear in themselves an almost tangible holiness. Awareness of the sacred, so terribly lacking in us moderns, arises spontaneously. When, within our own attitude, we thus restore the world to sacred order, we recognize Christ, the creative Word, in all things. Then joy fairly explodes into the most ordinary events. He is present in our smallest experience, as our newly meek eyes are able to see.

As noninjury deepens, we realize that this practice is a fresh way to practice love. The gentle kindness, the reverence, the harmony of kinship, the sense of sacredness, the recognition of Christ — all are aspects of love.

This new love may be a little different from love as we have previously experienced it. It is almost an impersonal kind of love, since it is the same for all. This love does not depend on the recipient but on our own practice, our own desire to be loving. That is exactly God's love, for it, too, is the same for all his creation.

So we change by persisting in this practice begun in Lent. We are more open. We are more tranquil. We respond more to God. We recognize God and receive his grace more easily and lastingly. We no longer place him at a distance with harsh feelings. With deeper closeness to God, of course there is joy — a joy that is deep and bright and remains long in the heart.

Practices

Following are questions for your reflection during Lent. Your answers will show you your own starting points for the practice of noninjury, realizing each person has to begin and the starting point is not all that important.

1. How do I presently do injury to myself or to others? In action? In words? In long-held feelings? In thoughts?
2. Exactly how do I feel inside when I might be injuring myself or another?
3. Do I believe I am justified in hurting another? Myself?
4. What one change can I make to begin the practice of noninjury?
5. How can I incorporate meekness into my prayers for joyful living?

Here are Scripture references to accompany your practice of noninjury.

Psalm 133:1-3
Psalm 141:1-4
Proverbs 3:3-4
Isaiah 52:7
Romans 12:14-21; 14:17-19
Hebrews 12:14
Matthew 5:7-9, 22-26, 38-45; 7:1-5; 18:21-35

CHAPTER 6

The Wonder of Contemplation

The path to joy is somewhat like an empty house: no matter which door or window you enter, you gain access to the whole house. All the practices we have been considering are doors and windows through which one can gain access to God's joy. We may enter through any of them. Now supposing we want to walk directly through the big front door. Do we have a key? Yes. That key is the daily practice of contemplation or centering prayer.

"Contemplation?" you may ask. "Isn't that a special gift of God reserved for very few?" Of course, it is a gift from God, and so is our breathing. It is not reserved for people different from you and me; God offers it to all of us.

Unfortunately, as Father Thomas Keating points out in his book *Open Mind, Open Heart,* for several hundred years the Church has given us the impression, indirectly as well as directly, that contemplative prayer is far beyond the reach of ordinary Christians. Now in this late twentieth century we are once again realizing that interior contemplative practice is the core of the deepest and best Christian life.

Recently, a friend was saying that he does not see how prayer without words, without reason, can get anywhere because "it's not logical." He is correct about "logic," but he is sadly mistaken about "getting anywhere." Contemplation is beyond logic, higher than reason, and closer to God than our thinking. It belongs to the realm of those qualities we all want: tranquillity, love, wonder, power, joy. None of these depends on logic or words. Cannot the lover gaze into the face of the beloved and be speechless, but happy? Does not peace fill us with quiet, where we need no thoughts? Do we not all experience moments of great wonder when it simply does not occur to us to need explanations?

So it is with God. "By love he may be touched and embraced, never by thought," says *The Cloud of Unknowing* (written by an unknown English mystic in the fourteenth century).[10]

What Is Contemplation?

What then is contemplation? Father William McNamara has called it a long loving look. Father Willigis Jager says the goal of contemplation is "to gaze upon the divine in ourselves...by means of an awareness that transcends our intellectual capabilities."[11]

Father Thomas Keating tells us it is "the opening of the mind and heart, body and emotions — our whole being — to God...beyond the psychological content of the present moment."[12] Love, openness, quietness, attention — these are the qualities of contemplative prayer. It is our alert, thought-free awareness of the center of our own being that is the image of God. Contemplation is much different from thinking.

There has been some confusion in recent years about the words contemplation and meditation. In traditional Christian usage, "meditation" has meant *reflection,* or *thinking,* about a subject, a Scripture passage, a person, or God. Contemplation has been understood to be that centering of the whole being on God, which leads to a transforming union with God. Contemplation is often said to be beyond thought and emotion.

In the Hindu and Buddhist tradition, the meaning of these two words is exactly reversed: meditation is beyond thought, and contemplation means thinking. The modern media, including the religious press, are not consistent. The reader must discover which kind of inner activity is intended in a particular discussion.

In these pages we follow traditional Christian usage and use "contemplation" for that effort to reach beyond thinking and emotions to God alone.

Ultimately, the greatest joy a human being can experience is the joy of union with God. To rest wholly in the loving heart of God is the goal of our existence as humans, the objective of our spiritual lives. It is the main thrust behind all that Jesus did and taught. To this joyful union, all who desire it are invited by the Lord.

The royal road to this most profound and mysterious of joys is contemplation. What we *do* to prepare ourselves for that deepest contemplation may be called *contemplative practice.* A practice is a technique that helps us receive what God wants to give — all of himself.

Do not think that we must already be perfect in order to begin contemplative practice. Contemplation will eventually perfect us if we persist in it. To begin, we need only the desire to do so.

The Practice of Contemplation

How do we practice contemplation? *The Cloud of Unknowing* describes perfectly the essence of our practice:

> Lift your heart up to the Lord, with a gentle stirring of love, desiring him for his own sake and not for his gifts. Center all your attention and desire on him and let this be the sole concern of your mind and heart. Do all in your power to forget everything else, keeping your thoughts and desires free from involvement with any of God's creatures or their affairs.[13]

Like so many interior efforts, this sounds perfectly clear (and easy) until we attempt it. The mind understands the words, but the rest of our being does not comprehend. We must practice how to "lift up our hearts," how to "center all our attention on God," how to "forget everything else."

Techniques — "how-tos" — abound. In the end, the simpler the method used, the better.

Four steps may be followed:

1. In an undisturbed place, try to find a comfortable position in which you can remain still for a while, with the spine straight if at all possible.

2. Take a few minutes to relax and quiet down from all busyness of the body and mind.

3. As you become a little more still, begin to repeat mentally a simple word or phrase you have chosen. Perhaps something like these suggestions: "Jesus." "I love you." "Hail, Mary."

4. When thoughts and feelings arise, do not resist them, but return your attention quietly to your prayer phrase.

Let's look at each of these steps.

First, the position of the body is important chiefly because it can be a major distraction if you do not take care of it. If the spine is not straight, you will squirm. If it is straight, it will support the body almost effortlessly. Many who practice contemplation in the East sit cross-legged. *For them* it is a comfortable position with a straight spine. Few Westerners can manage it without long practice. For most of us, a chair is best, with feet flat on the floor, hands in the lap. The back may be supported.

Experiment to find the most comfortable and supported position. Even lying down is fine. Only it is not recommended that you try it on the bed (or any other oh-so-soft spot)!

Second, it is vital to give yourself a few minutes to calm down. Contemplative practice is not possible for a racing mind and a scattered attention. To quiet yourself, sit still, take a few deep, long breaths, and let the body relax. One may check mentally various muscles: the toes, the thighs, the shoulders, fingers, and face. Are they all resting? Some people focus on a picture, a candle, or listen to a chant on tape for a few minutes. The rule here is simple: Use whatever works for you.

Personally, I find it easiest to be quiet first thing in the morning, before my mind gets totally "revved up." I get up before the world is noisy, wash my face, do a few stretches, and then sit for contemplative practice. Although many people find this just-out-of-bed time the best for quiet, others find it impossible. The time is not so important, except that just after meals is usually not good. Again, whatever helps you, whatever time is good for you, should be followed.

Whichever time, it is useful to practice every day at the same time and in the same place and position. The body will get in the habit of being still at that time and place. It will eventually settle down on its own, and the mind will soon follow.

Third, when quieter, begin to repeat your chosen prayer, phrase, or word. Father Basil Pennington and Father Thomas Keating prefer a single, simple word. Over the centuries many repetitive formulas have been used effectively. Perhaps the best known is the Jesus Prayer, which in its simplest version is "Jesus Christ, have mercy on me." Words like love or peace or holy names like Jesus, Mary, or Yahweh may also be chosen.

A prayer phrase should be attractive and comfortable. It should have a positive meaning, or none at all, because it is going to drop deeply into our being with constant repetition. It should not be a word that starts a long train of thought, but it may have pleasant, warm associations.

Once chosen, stay with the same word or phrase. Hopping around keeps the practice superficial. Do not reflect on this prayer phrase. Simply repeat it attentively and quietly in your mind.

Fourth, when thoughts enter, when emotions arise, when you suddenly become aware that you are far, far away, then gently return to your prayer phrase. Do not fight these distractions. They will be there anyway for many years. When we fight them, they actually get stronger. Pay as little attention to them as possible, letting them come and go as they will. Return your focus to your prayer phrase as often as you need to. Sister Ludwigis, a Benedictine nun, told us that if we return to our phrase five hundred times in a single contemplative practice period, we have had a wonderful time! The point is our return, not the fact of distractions.

All four of these steps have to do with training our attention to forget everything except the Lord. To try to forget one's world is like being told, "For three minutes now, do not think of a pink elephant." Try it. You'll find you can hardly think of anything else. But when we focus on what we want to attend to, the other things drop out of our awareness. So, by means of our prayer phrase, we focus on God and gradually we do forget all else.

Contemplation and Lent

If we begin a contemplative practice as a Lenten effort, we may well find that we want to keep doing it after Lent is over. The side effects of contemplation are very attractive: we are more peaceful, we are stronger, we love more, we react less violently to life. We feel closer to God because we are closer to God. We taste joys springing up from within our hearts, often unexpectedly. In fact, it has been said, "Sit daily for contemplative practice and the rest of your life will take care of itself." It sounds far-fetched, but I testify to my own experiences of its truth.

Experiences, strange or familiar, may or may not happen during our practice itself. If they do, it is best to give quiet thanks and return to our prayer phrase. Saint John of the Cross advised us not to look for particular experiences in contemplation itself. They may or may not come. He told us to be alert instead to what is happening in our lives. When an emergency comes along, we may handle it better than before. We may experience unfamiliar peacefulness right in the middle of our busyness or even in pain or unhappiness. Our relationships may begin to seem increasingly patient and loving. If, little by ever so little, we begin to grow into the image of Christ that is already within us, we know our contemplative practice is bearing fruit.

If we do not notice any particular changes, we are urged to proceed in trust that God is at work in us. Often enough, God's work goes on, hidden and silent in our depths, until we are ready to perceive it more directly.

If we continue to practice contemplation, it will become more and more important to us. Although in the beginning we may have to insist with ourselves to practice daily, in time we feel lost if we do not sit for contemplation. A sign of this shift may be a new awareness of how noisy and distracting many of our activities are.

For example, I long ago discovered that if I see a movie in the evening, my morning practice is a rerun. When I noticed that, I had to choose: rerun or contemplation? There was nothing intrinsically wrong with a good movie, but it got in the way of my quiet with God. So I choose to not watch movies in the evening but instead go to matinees. I do my rerun before sleeping and then forget it.

Similarly, we may find that many activities undermine our contemplative practice while others support it. As each one comes to our attention, we are free to decide how we want to respond. The choice we make will tell us what is truly the most important to us — a very valuable piece of self-knowledge.

In general, activities that highly stimulate mind or body make contemplative practice more difficult. Activities that encourage quiet or relaxation or openness will support our contemplation. For myself, classical music, being out in nature, good exercise, craft work, eating moderately, and such are supportive. Television, loud music, lots of traffic noise, hurrying, talking too much, any tension-producing activities — these make contemplative practice very difficult.

We depend on the help of the Holy Spirit. Indeed, deepening our contemplation is the most directly transformative work the Spirit does. As we experience the gradual, lovely changes in ourselves and our lives, we notice that weaving in and out of everything is a bright thread of joy. It plays hide-and-seek with us, to be sure, but when it hides, we know that it will again appear. As Jesus said, the Spirit goes where it wills, in perfect freedom. But Teilhard de Chardin reminds us that "joy is the infallible sign of the presence of God." When God enters our awareness, joy is always known.

Practices

Here are exercises you may wish to try to help yourself relax and sense a growing tranquillity of mind:

1. Gaze long out the window and watch the clouds float in the sky.
2. Go for a long walk at dawn or early evening. Notice what your eyes, nose, and ears report to you. Simply notice.
3. Do a jigsaw puzzle, in quiet — no background sounds.
4. Listen to peaceful music. Do not read or do anything else. Listen only.
5. Sing a simple melody over and over for twenty minutes or so. "Peace Is Flowing Like a River" is a good one for this.
6. Get a massage. Sink into the lovely relaxation of it.
7. Watch a child play or a cat live its cat-day.
8. Get up at 2:00 a.m. and go outside; feel the night.
9. Forgive someone from your heart.
10. Take out your snapshots of a vacation. Relax and relive its pleasures.
11. Walk slowly, attentively, noticing every move of foot muscles, every readjustment of weight.
12. Fold paper and cut out snowflakes.
13. For one day refrain from resentment.
14. Practice your contemplation in the company of a good friend who also practices contemplation.

Following are Scripture passages for your reflection.
Deuteronomy 6:5
Psalms 19:15, 34:6-9; 103:1-22; 116:7-9;
  119:15, 16, 27, 30-32, 47-48; 130:5-6; 131:1-3
Isaiah 30:15; 40:31
Matthew 6:6-8
John 3:29-30; 15:4-5
2 Corinthians 5:17, 21

CHAPTER 7

Discipline:
Freedom for Joy

I f you have experimented sincerely with any of the practices offered in this book, you have discovered that they are not fully possible at the first attempt. Perhaps you are surprised that they require practice. Such practice is a discipline. It requires effort to direct mind and body to attain any goal we seek. That goal is joy in God that only the Spirit can give but that we must be able to hold. We know that attainment in any field requires discipline. The athlete must train, the scholar must study, the artist must practice. Should the attainment of joy challenge us any less than these?

Like other wonderful words, "discipline" has acquired a nasty connotation for some of us. We may think of it as punishment or as an unwanted obligation to keep rules we find unattractive or simply the necessity of doing things we would prefer not to do. We may feel that discipline will interrupt our comforts and pleasures.

It is true that certain pleasures may be interrupted or even left completely aside when we turn willingly to self-discipline. Those pleasures are not cut out of us, leaving us empty, but rather, they are transcended. In place of each one, a much deeper and more lasting quality enters our experience. If we want to keep any of the life experiences we cherish, discipline is required. If we want to live joyfully most of the time, discipline is necessary.

Discipline implies effort, and sometimes we resist that effort. In nature there is a principle called "entropy." Simply, it means that whatever sits still is deteriorating. If something is not growing, it is decaying. There is in nature no such thing as staying the same. So also in our human life. If we are not climbing upward, we are sliding backward. Climbing upward requires definite effort.

Discipline always implies inner friction (will I or won't I?). Especially in the beginning, the friction may be experienced as unpleasant. That simply shows that our senses or our minds do not always find discipline comfortable or easy.

Yet we know that if we do not discipline children, they will grow wild and tangled inside. We, too, if we are undisciplined, will be unclear and weak, perhaps subject to the passing whim of every fad, every commercial on television, every person's opinion.

Almost everyone has experienced the pain of feeling the need for a particular capacity for a particular thing, but not having it. Here are two of mine. You may wish to recall and ponder your own.

Some years ago a dear friend found herself in great pain. I knew that the most powerful thing that I could do for her would be to start a long period of intense intercessory prayer. So I began. Almost immediately I found that I could maintain prayer for a short time only. Then willy-nilly, I would wander away to other things. How I wished I had kept a prayer discipline so that in this moment I could truly help my friend.

Again, when I was a new Catholic, the opportunity came for my first "hour of adoration" before the Blessed Sacrament. I wondered what one "does" for a whole hour. Talking with others, I heard that one does spiritual reading, reads traditional prayers, says words to God (hopefully from the heart), praises God, makes intentions, and so on. These, however, did not seem enough. I sensed that "adoration" could be an uninterrupted period of profound loving attention to the Lord. But try as I did, I was not able to do that.

Freedom and Strength

As we have already noted, our experiences of joy or love or peace do not stay with us. They pass all too quickly and leave us with wistful longing for them to come again.

Why? Why can we not hold the experience of God? Why can we not pray as deeply, as steadily, as we wish? Why is our experience of joy so fleeting? It's because we lack two qualities that only discipline can give us: freedom and strength.

"Ah, if I could only get away to an island somewhere, with no pressures and no routine, pick fruit from everbearing trees, and have the time to do as I wish...."

So goes a familiar fantasy. We know that it is not realistic, but we may feel that it is unreal only because we lack money. The real fallacy, however, is more likely a vague assumption that freedom is doing as I please at every moment and that this kind of freedom produces happiness. It does sound good, but it is not true. Pressure-free, structureless lives are not free at all. The freedom to experience the quality of life we desire is rooted quite differently in human beings.

Freedom that brings happiness is not freedom-from. It is freedom-to. That is, we become happy, as we are free to live in ways that allow us to know the joy and peace of God's own grace. Freedom to live in a certain way is not "to do as I please all the time." It is, rather, freedom grounded in interior strength and flexibility, and especially inner trust and calm reliance on God's generosity. This true freedom begins within us; it is found within us and grows within us. Freedom blossoms first in our own interior self and with our own attitudes.

It's an old story, but it illustrates this point. A wealthy woman was vacationing in New York City, paying a high price for a good room in a famous hotel. One evening, from the suite next door, came loud piano-playing. But it was not music; it was endless scales and exercises, banged out with entirely too much verve. It irritated her greatly. She stormed down to the manager and demanded that the noise be stopped, that the person move to another room.

The manager looked sympathetic and said, "I'm sorry, I cannot move your neighbor. But I will be happy to have our staff help you move to another room, just as nice, and as quiet as you wish." Well, she did not think that was fair, but if it was the only possibility, she would move, grudgingly. Certainly, she did not want to live with all that racket!

"By the way," the manager said, "it may interest you to know that the man playing scales is Paderewski." The woman's mouth fell open. In a flash she decided not to change rooms. Soon she had invited several friends to join her and listen to the great pianist practice.

It is rarely the circumstance, almost always the attitude, that determines the way we experience a situation. The feeling of freedom is like that. It is an interior state, independent of the nature of our circumstances. That is why the fantasy island-life is an illusion.

The inner feeling of freedom depends on a disciplined mind and heart, as well as a keen body. The freedom to dance gloriously on a stage rests on much intense discipline. The freedom to pray effectively for another person is available only when prayer is already a strong disciplined practice. The freedom to spend an hour actually adoring God takes great strength and attentiveness, the result only of inner discipline. The freedom to accept the joy of God depends on the strength given by disciplined living.

The Necessity of Discipline

Discipline implies order; it implies a regulated life, a life that is lived according to some rule. When a person becomes a "disciple" in any field, a teacher or master is followed who knows that field. The teacher gives the disciple an order to follow, tailored to fit both the goal and the particular disciple.

Just as each child needs a somewhat different form of discipline, so each disciple's needs differ a little, even when the goal is shared. A basis common to all Christians is the moral demand of the Ten Commandments. Yet "having a religion" or "following the precepts" does not necessarily mean a person is a disciple. The disciple, truly opening to freedom and joy, accepts more discipline than the minimum. Precisely what is required beyond the common basics varies for each individual.

Some will need definite physical practices, like fasting. Others may find that disciplining other actions is more helpful, by doing or avoiding certain behavior. Some people need to discipline their emotional lives, others their thoughts. Perhaps we all need to grow in each of these areas, but the proportions of each practice will vary.

One is not a disciple until one gladly accepts the discipline involved. One must love the discipline itself, as well as the Master.

Loving the Master, one knows that the support of Jesus is present within us. Loving the discipline, the inner world will open itself to the strength of God. The disciple accepts this discipline, not as an unwelcome restriction but as an open path leading directly to the desired goal. If our goal is the top of a mountain, we'll want to take the more direct route. We do not wander all over every fascinating meadow along the way. If we persist, one step at a time, we will find ourselves in the glory of the peak, nothing between us and the sky. Looking back, we see that each step has been as important as the previous one and the all-important final one.

To be effective, discipline must be wholeheartedly accepted. An imposed order, followed only reluctantly, accomplishes little. I recall an incident that happened when I had been a Catholic for about four months. It was August 15, the Solemnity of the Assumption of Our Lady. A young woman working one floor up from my office was also Catholic. I went to her and wished her a happy feast day. She looked at me blankly for a moment, then said (and I quote exactly), "Oh, I almost forgot. That's another thing I've got to do today!" This discipline was imposed, and somewhat grudgingly accepted. It more than likely did not help her to receive God's joy that day.

Deeper discipline is a regulating of life, which we welcome happily and freely because it leads to our goal. Such an open attitude changes our experience of the discipline. Thus our particular practices must originate within us, not in an external imposition. That is, though we may not invent a practice (the best ones are already known), we follow it fully because it resonates with our deeper inner desires. If it does not, we likely will not even persist in it.

Discipline implies a certain generosity, a self-giving to the practice we have chosen. It means that we will do it, even when our bodies would rather not, even when we don't feel like it or when it seems to be giving us nothing in return. Rewards are not always immediate, but they definitely do arrive. We give ourselves in action and in attitude to our practice, trusting to God for the results in joy that we desire. Such generosity will test our limits and reveal our weaknesses to us, but this is a necessary part of discipline's purpose in our growth.

Discipline implies regularity. It means that we choose our practice (or accept it from a teacher), and then we do it every day. It does little good to practice once, then forget it for several days, then try to practice for another couple days, and so on. Only consistent effort brings the rewards. We know this perfectly well in athletics. Baseball players practice daily; weightlifters do their lifting daily; professional golfers try to play each day, even in the rain.

The strength that comes with discipline shows itself in many ways. We may simply feel stronger, more able to live this life. We may notice that when circumstances do not go our way, we meet them with more poise. Our relationships may improve. We may find that we are increasingly able to accomplish a change we have long wanted to make.

Perhaps the clearest demonstration of our new disciplined strength appears in a crisis. The person who has lived a certain daily rule, interiorly and outwardly, is strengthened by that very practice when there is great challenge or great pain. Griefs have not only been survived but used for growth by those whose lives already included some kind of discipline. Even when the body is ill or relationships difficult or when too many changes occur too fast, the one who practices a daily discipline will continue to practice, and it will be a strength and a solace for the troubled times.

All of us experience a little discipline by force of circumstances — a joy we must do every day or responsibilities to which we must respond. This kind of discipline does strengthen us, especially if we welcome it as a positive factor and allow it to give power and strength to our living. In addition the high level of our goal will ask of us that we heartily undertake a particular goal-oriented discipline.

So for the strength and freedom required to receive joy, our living must be disciplined. Any of the practices here recommended can be undertaken as daily discipline.

When we begin to discipline ourselves toward joy, it is important that we not begin with too much. If we try to start too many new things at once, we are certain to feel unhappy with ourselves when we cannot maintain them. It is better to begin with a smaller effort that we know we can sustain. For some of us, myself included, it is important that the first efforts are also a little challenging. If they are not, people often get bored and quit. So we begin with something that attracts us, something that is not too much nor too easy.

Practices

The practices in this book — and any other effective Lenten practices — can provide those three elements. So when choosing a plan for your Lenten discipline, pray about these questions: Does this attract me? Is it within reach and within reason for me? Is there enough challenge in it? Do not rush the answers. Trust your inner inclination as reliable advice from the Lord and begin to practice. We need to create a good balance in our efforts, but we can afford to teeter a little until we discover our own point of equilibrium.

For example, an hour of daily contemplative practice may sound attractive, but you also have three preschoolers and a sick parent. Is that a challenge? Of course it is, and it is probably too much. Perhaps you might begin with fifteen minutes each morning. Keep that fifteen-minute period regardless.

If you are in the midst of a sad and unfulfilling marriage, the practice of contentment may sound wonderful, but you may not be able to approach it without changing your circumstances. You are better off to begin with one of the other practices that you can sustain in your present situation.

Perhaps noninjury sounds perfectly awful to you because you

are angry and confused from past experiences and choices. You may not want to practice noninjury. Then you can choose another practice that you can love.

In order to find the discipline most beneficial to you, you must begin where you are. You must take into account your present capacities, your present liabilities, what attracts you and what does not attract you. God is where you are, and if you seek him at all, you always seek him from where you actually are. You cannot go to some other place to start.

If you are sincere in your wish for Lenten joy in God, you must begin a loving discipline, and you must keep it consistently. Only when the Spirit has done its work through discipline in you, will you find yourself free enough and strong enough to experience and hold the joy you desire.

Here are Scripture passages for your support.
Psalm 119:129-135
Proverbs 3:11-12, 29-30; 4:23-27
Matthew 6:13-14
1 Corinthians 9:24-27
Galatians 6:9
James 1:2-4
Hebrews 12:7-13

CONCLUSION

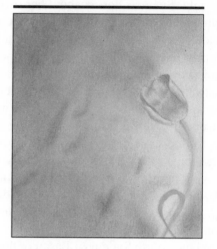

Joy for Lent — Joy Forever

I n the beginning of this book, we noted that Lent is meant to be a time to emphasize change, and that the change that comes is hoped to last. If Lent is for disciplined effort to cooperate with the transformative work of the Holy Spirit, then Easter certainly will have more meaning than ever before.

Once a friend told me she felt badly because she could not seem to feel sad on Good Friday, and she was not especially happy on

Easter. She thought something was wrong with her faith. I thought something was right. She was honest about her own feelings, and she could not pretend to have a feeling she did not have. The only mistake she made was to berate herself for natural feelings and a natural experience. We are hardly expected to create feelings because we think they are somehow "supposed" to be there.

Nevertheless, a lack of connection to these great feast days may indicate that our previous observing of them was a bit skewed or out-of-synch. Certainly, if we do the same thing every Lent, or different things for the same old reasons, after a few years it may become just another routine. It is my experience, though, that if every Lent brings a more profound practice than the one before, each one is new. Each time our life becomes deeper and our relationship to God closer. That makes Easter Sunday an especially wonderful, happy celebration.

But what about the Fourth Sunday of Easter or the Tenth Sunday in Ordinary Time? Does our Easter experience last? To the extent that it is only emotion, it will not last. Insofar as it might represent a turning point in our ongoing transformation, its significance will last. Can the opening of our heart to joy become continual? Yes, if we wish to continue those practices that support an opening heart.

First, ponder intently what you already know (or will discover if you practice with this book). Our longing for joy is actually our longing for God, to be one with God. If we search with particularly focused intention during this Lent, much will open to us that we will not want to abandon on Easter Monday. We may think of it as a search for joy or a search for transformation in the Holy Spirit or a search for union with God — the words matter little. What does matter is that we may wish to continue.

Continuing will itself be a joyful experience if we allow it to be so. Perhaps on Easter this year, we can rededicate ourselves to continue the practice we have undertaken or to begin another experience for the next season. Our rededication should not take the form of an absolute resolution. That kind of resolution is bound to be broken and we'll only feel guilty, and our loving Lord never instructs us to feel guilty.

Instead, take some time during Holy Week to review your Lent. Use these last days of Lent as a quiet time to get completely clear about what you want this coming year to bring to you inwardly. If you have practiced contentment, you may hope that it remains as a constant state of experience. If you have practiced contemplation, you may want to pray that way from now on. If you have undertaken to explore noninjury, you may find it too beautiful to let go. Choose what you want to maintain inside. Recall that this gift you want is in God and offer your renewed desire to him. Ask him to show you how to keep going.

When we seek this clarity, we are asking ourselves what we care about most keenly. No practice will give us true fruit if we do it only mechanically. We must care about it. In this age of technological innovation, it is especially tempting to believe that if we perform the right actions, push the correct buttons, results are assured. Technique is necessary, yes, but the power is in the caring heart that acts through the method. Our caring about joy, about God, will draw him to us. Our methods are aimed at preparing us for his "arrival." Our techniques help us receive him.

The practices outlined in this book are founded less on method than on caring. We either care or we learn to care when we practice noninjury or surrender. We either love contemplation or learn to love it. We find the journey interesting in the beginning and learn to care about it along the way. Unless that happens, the practices become more than practices. They become ourselves, exactly the way we are in life.

As joy increasingly accompanies these practices, joy becomes increasingly our stance through every event of our lives. As we experience God more and more, we become consciously aware that

God is in the air and he is the light by which we live our lives. Then we know the "practice" has moved more deeply within us and we are created anew.

Looking ahead, then, to growth and change as we continue our practices toward joy, are there hints of how to proceed? Here are two.

Continue the Practices

One is to practice in all our seasons, in all our moods, in all our circumstances — home, work, play, rest. We know this, yet we so easily fall into compartmentalizing our living. The compartment for God is not always the biggest either. I was forcibly reminded of this once when my usual life, built around my practices, was seriously interrupted. I had to leave home and live in less congenial circumstances for about a month, with heavy responsibilities. Now you may think that one who dares to write a book like this always sees her own life perfectly. Not so! I was upset that my daily routine of practices would be impossible for this time. Then a friend wished me well, "as you continue your journey in your coming situation...."

It hit me hard. I had been letting my practice depend on circumstances. Now here were new circumstances, but the thread of my living journey was the same. There was no need to pause, no threat to real inner practice. Only a few adjustments needed to be made in the how of it all and the conscious practices went on quite powerfully — much to my surprise.

By this I learned what I pass along to you. Whatever you choose to practice, attempt to do it in all circumstances, interiorly, hidden if necessary. You can always find a way to continue if you want to do so. No circumstance needs to keep you from God, from his joy, if you are established within your heart where God dwells. Long-term practices are aimed exactly at attaining this inner established state.

The second suggestion: little by little, examine your lifestyle and all its parts and ask this question: Does *this* habit (or pleasure or activity or work or friend or...) support my continued practice? Does it hinder it? John Woolman, a great American Quaker saint in the 1700s, resolved to leave behind everything in his life that did not actively contribute to his spiritual journey. He organized his life around this principle with extraordinary thoroughness. It affected his textile business, his relationships, his church life, even the clothes he wore.

We may not be able to be as definite or as thorough as John Woolman was, but his example can inspire us to gradually bring our lives under the same microscope. At least we can try and we will know what we are doing to our spiritual possibility. When we know that, we can choose each item of our days. In this choice there is immense power. We become aware of our lives and our capacity to mold them for God. In this newly recognized strength, joy appears again and again. We become, in our own eyes, no longer victims of our habits but, increasingly, *actual* children of God, playing in joy.

If we choose to keep moving toward joy, beginning with this Easter, we will make yet another discovery in our own experience. Wherever we enter, by whatever practice, if continued in a disciplined way, we will gradually be given access to a wonder-filled life in God. Even if we come into this kingdom by a hidden back road, the whole kingdom will lie open to be explored, to be claimed as our own home.

As our exploration continues by means of ever-deepening practices, our interior capacities are enlarged both by practice and by God's constant alertness to us, by his grace poured into our practice. Our hope — and the glorious possibility for everyone who sincerely desires it — is God himself. Meister Eckhart puts it perfectly:

As the powers of the soul become more perfect and unmixed, so they apprehend more perfectly and comprehensively whatever they apprehend, receiving it more comprehensively, having greater joy...to the point where the highest power of the soul receives into itself nothing less than God himself, in all the vastness and fullness of his being....There is no delight and no joy that can be compared with this union and this fulfilling and this joy.[14]

May God in his mercy grant us the grace of this joy in him, during this, our present life — and forever!

Notes

[1] Bengt Hoffman, editor. *The Theologia Germanica of Martin Luther* (NY: Paulist Press, 1980), page 67.

[2] C.J. De Catanzaro. *Symeon, the New Theologian: The Discourses* (NY: Paulist Press, 1980), page 181.

[3] Edmund Colledge, O.S.A., and Bernard McGinn, translators. *Meister Eckhart: The Essential Sermons, Commentaries, Treatises and Defense* (NY: Paulist Press, 1981), page 179.

[4] Mary T. Clark, translator. *Augustine of Hippo: Selected Writings* (NY: Paulist Press, 1984), page 85.

[5] Colledge and McGinn, op. cit., page 230.

[6] Evelyn Underhill. *Mysticism* (NY: New American Library, 1955), page 206.

[7] Colledge and McGinn, op. cit., page 43.

[8] Colledge and McGinn, op. cit., page 260.

[9] Walter Hilton, translated by M.L. Del Mastro. *The Stairway of Perfection* (Garden City, NY: Image Books, 1979), page 156.

[10] William Johnston, editor. *The Cloud of Unknowing and the Book of Privy Counselling* (Garden City, NY: Doubleday Image Books, 1973), page 54.

[11] Willigis Jager, Jr., translated by Matthew J. O'Connell. *The Way to Contemplation: Encountering God Today* (Mahwah, NJ: Paulist Press, 1987), page 3.

[12] Thomas Keating. *Open Mind, Open Heart* (Warwick, NY: Amity House, 1986), page 14.

[13] Johnston, op. cit., page 48.

[14] Colledge and McGinn, op. cit., page 220.

More from Marilyn Norquist Gustin...

THE BEATITUDES
Jesus' Pattern for a Happy Life

Invites you to consider the beatitudes as a pattern for speech — a plan that *can* be followed in today's world. This book advises us to be quiet and listen to what Jesus said in the Sermon on the Mount — when he gave us a pattern for daily life and a way to face troubles and problems and still find peace, hope, and joy. **$3.95**

HOW TO READ AND PRAY THE GOSPELS

This book was written to help you understand the message of the gospels and to help you *pray* the Scriptures. It offers prayer suggestions, ideas for family use, and questions for discussion. **$2.50**

FROM VICTIM TO DECISION-MAKER
Keys to Personal Growth

This book presents a joyful, faith-filled vision of our own power of choice. You'll discover the keys to the small steps that, over time, can help you move from a victim of circumstance to decision-maker. The author also includes points for personal reflection and suggests helpful Scripture readings. **$1.95**

Order from your local bookstore or write to
Liguori Publications
Box 060, Liguori, MO 63057-9999
*(Please add $1.00 for postage and handling
for orders under $5.00; $1.50 for orders over $5.00.)*